I0457803

love letters to the wild

JANET MACFADYEN

DOS MADRES

2025

DOS MADRES PRESS INC.

P.O. Box 294, Loveland, Ohio 45140
www.dosmadres.com   editor@dosmadres.com

Dos Madres is dedicated to the belief that the small press is essential
to the vitality of contemporary literature as a carrier of the new voice,
as well as the older, sometimes forgotten voices of the past. And in an
ever more virtual world, to the creation of fine books pleasing to the
eye and hand.

Dos Madres is named in honor of Vera Murphy and Libbie Hughes,
the "Dos Madres" whose contributions have made this press possible.

Dos Madres Press, Inc. is an Ohio Not For Profit Corporation and a
501 (c) (3) qualified public charity. Contributions are tax deductible.

Executive Editor: Robert J. Murphy

Illustration & Book Design: Elizabeth H. Murphy
www.illusionstudios.net

Cover and author photos by Stephen H. Schmidt

Typeset in Adobe Garamond Pro & Killigraphy
ISBN 978-1-962847-35-3
Library of Congress Control Number: 2025945851

First Edition
Copyright 2025 Janet MacFadyen
All rights reserved. No part of this book may be reproduced or transmitted in
any form or by any means graphic, electronic or mechanical, including photo-
copying, recording, taping or by any information storage or retrieval system,
without the permission in writing from the publisher.
Published by Dos Madres Press, Inc.

GRATITUDE

I am deeply indebted to the returning residences at the Fine Arts Work Center, along with residencies at Wellspring House and Cill Rialaig, for the time and inspiration to complete this manuscript. Big thank you to my readers: Carolyn Cushing, Mary Gilliland, Kat Good-Schiff, Gian Lombardo, Dorothy McFarland, Robin Morris, Kim Port Parsons, Mary Clare Powell, Ed Rayher, and Maria Williams; and to Robert and Elizabeth Murphy for ushering this work into the world.

Finally, in a time when our public lands are under siege, I want to express my gratitude for the existence of the following irreplaceable landscapes that inspired many of these poems: the Cape Cod National Seashore, Death Valley National Park, Yosemite National Park, and Pictured Rocks National Lakeshore; and to the many many local conservation areas for continuing the hard work of preserving wild areas close to home.

For Steve, as always

TABLE OF CONTENTS

love letters to the wild

Dear Storm Clouds,

Please accept these poems: sand and bone, ochre and ash. We have been running up and down on paved switchbacks, our only path through sharks fins of stone, hued peach and olive-green — a giant gravel pit. My hat goes flying, rain drops flying. Pelting wind and sunlight, eardrums popping, all of us blinded, bombarded with images with no context. No sorting mechanism to separate the borax from salt, salt from bone.

Is this ecstasy or devastation? We stare and stare, but all we see are the nos: no potable water, no flushable water, no water in the sinks except badwater. No easy exit. No understanding of water spitting down from the sky like manna.

Didn't you say all this was ours?

Dear Storm Clouds,

We have been walking, and now we are below sea level. The ocean has long since dried up, leaving only its salt. I see a thin bush greening against the gravel outwash.

A black bird flew over an ashen hill. A plant of pubic hair swirled out of the white precipitant.

Once there were mule teams. Once there was money but no food. Now, who are these strangers beside us, the woman in the wheelchair, the person gripping the handrail?

So silent my ears sting. Distant cars shuttle back and forth between a ridge of brown ash, ridge of acid sand. Giant prone figures, the ancient women of the hills. They have instructions, but we can't read their expression. We need to learn braille, trust our fingers for the way forward.

Can our eyes open?

Isn't it time we all   The sun is setting in earnest. There is so little time.

Isn't it time we

A moth flits in the dim. A painted van — some kind of message on its side —makes its way down, tires scrunching. Its doors open and shut; then it proceeds slowly into the half-light. Two motorcyclists idle side by side, kicking up dust. They follow the van and vanish.

Two dark forms on bicycles appear and disappear. Perhaps we are half-awake, o storm clouds, we need a story to make sense of the information.

Desolation, Indifference, Devotion.

The moth is back, lands on my shirtsleeve. A profound silence between us. Everything is connected. Two people walk down the gravel track following the motorcycles, two dark figures on foot. Two by two the animals —

Have you seen the ark beached like a whale? Its bleached ribs are sticking up just over there.

Storm Clouds are you there? Today some vast painter has layered the ground in color: chlorite for blue/green, iron for red, titanium and magnesium for white. Has brushed calligraphy on a cliff, lilac on a flaking rock.

Volcanic upwellings. The earth heaves and pants giving birth, the vibrant earth, molten core, heart beating against the warm caress of my hand. Did you see the two little tow-headed girls giggling on an iron boulder, waving their skirts, showing their panties?

Did I tell you about the man walking his dog on that distant ridge? Only it was not his dog, it was his shadow that dogged him.

O dear storm clouds where are you? What can we scry with these piled crystals? We walk on them for miles in something close to joy, fading in, fading out against the expanse of — sugar or salt? Coarse-grained. No one is eating it. Now we arrive at the lowest point — there are a hundred cars and a bus and a parking lot.

Dried cracked mud bleeding salt. There are so many cracks through which to bleed: nerve frets, blood vessels, wounds. The brown legs of the mother crazed with ritual lines, a white tracery. A Babel of languages, a confusion, except all of us follow the same white river into the haze. There appears to be no other way. You could say, we are going the way of the lemmings.

But I cannot take my eyes off the glittering diamonds, dancing with molecules. It's hard not to leave the body, not to evaporate into the air.

A layer cake is sliced on the bias and disassembled, but there is no piece for us. Money begets money: a basin pours golden gullies off its golden spines. Frozen motion. Stones come alive. We are riding a sea of shifting sediments while we sleep!

I saw a dragonfly, I saw a moth. Saw a line of twinkling headlights coming down the 3,000 foot drop. Travelers all pooling at the bottom. Slow drop, slow motion. Things always in flux, always connected.

I would write something more to you, Storm Clouds, if I could pry more chalk out of the rock. If the sun were not blazing overhead, too bright to see.

Does waking wake the terrors — sunstroke and freezing, getting lost, starvation? Or wake the ecstasies? Too high, too exposed, frenzied, disoriented, enraptured. For god's sake, get me down to where

Behold, a sign: Go There☞ a rough wash in a waterless land. Place-holder etched by ancient flood. Cobblestones to stumble on. Is Noah still out there? We will walk seeking, we try not to succumb,

we remain yours —

I am a parched forest

We have no bodies other than light
No heart other than sunlight rippling across our trunks

No words

except for cricket wings, these shoulder blades
rubbing and rubbing

I don't know why — this dried up stream, this
broken branch of a life

The pools that fed us
dry and crack, the ancient sunlight

massages and massages the tired skin
until it breaks open,

land sucked clean of succor & something from within
cries Replenish me

& something from without
cries Nothing is enough, give me more & more

Do you understand? I am a hollowed log, a drum
I leave my body

in the drummer's hands

Dream oasis

Through the trees, an immense lake.
At the lake's edge, a cliff. On the lip

of the cliff, a beach. The sand,
the cliff face, the waves: some

mistake has been made— someone
left the beach stranded

in the air; someone
forgot to lift the sea to the shore.

The sky is perfect, the lake
serene, the beach white and smooth

on its sandstone perch.
What are we to make of so much

water nearby, a dream of abundance?
The oasis has grown huge, it has flooded

my dreams, washed up on my shore— blue
and aqua and aquamarine.

Scrub oak, pitch pine

Let me be
so alive as these
desiccated leaves
moving all their lives
from mold to salt,
wind to wind.
And look! a pitch
pine's boa-
constrictored limbs
drape over us,
wrap around what-
ever they claim—air
and its blueness, ar-
thritic-fingered oaks, all
unnoticed until
we sit on this
split rail fence
grayed out from
salt and moisture.
We are of
this world, fashioned
of salt and breath.
May we be
as patient as this
old one next to
me, whose lower
branches grip
its spent bleached
cones, be-
wreathed with lichen

—also gray—a smoky
pitch pine, gray-
thumbed, gray-eared
listening
with quiet
memory.

How I walk into my life

I go out on the deck with my cup
to ask the high sky and towering pines
who are you, you great silent watchers?
How do I open myself to gratitude?
How do I lay myself down for seedlings to take root?
How shall I not grind down
the teeming cities under my heels,
the microbes and mycelium, lives
too tiny for my Jupiter eyes? Tell me,
is the world full? Does it ask of me blessings?
Or is it a living engine unto itself and I
left speechless behind, I a world
but not in control of the world? Look,
see what insects fly out of my mouth,
what stingers and burrowing hands, the threads
of twined blood vessel and fungi
spinning the root basket of my ribs.

We find ourselves born here

There's a tree on the hilltop

with three braided trunks
like a bread loaf and long

fertile slit — everything else
dried and rustling except

this ancient being who urges up

quivering chipmunks, a bird
with ratcheting call, vanishing

back of a vixen. The hour

skips quietly ahead, humming
like a girl on the back route to home

through field and meadowsweet,
cloaked in mist and who knows

what thoughts that vanish
into the welcoming trees — all

that has come to pass and all

that is approaching —

sorrow and smoke
tangled up in the branches.

Everything we thought familiar emerges utterly strange

Skiffs stacked like fish on ice
The ranger's station with boat trailer wood stove wood rack
Road slicked with mud, the wind
shaking clouds off its back, wind
waking up

Small birds
flit over frozen grass, two dead outboard motors, the inboard heat
of our bodies burning,
four eyes two souls, the wind's
one mind giving utterance, drawing quantities of air
into its shimmering lungs
ever restless
plotting

The wind
voices my complaints, various and
insignificant, nags at my back, it wants
out, it wants
us to listen, becomes us when we are not thinking, when we
are porous as sponges,
laps from around an embankment, sighs beautifully
its eyes closed, its hair
streaming with cirrus cloud, streams of charged particles
ions protons neutrinos quarks sparkles of light glints
of flint flying in blue air, chips of ice
teeth of the wind, mouth ballooning

coming in on the northwest
a storm yes
a storm with snow in its maw

We huddle down, try to preserve heat, preserve
kindliness among bits of glass, the chains
yanking against guard posts, everything
rattling, everything pressed

Our bodies
break open, wind
roaring through our lungs

Love letters to the wild

Yes, I did weep. Yes
we painted the walls of our living
room with a smoldering red, like the urge

to shatter the sheetrock. The crumpled
letters, wood stove creaking
from its effort of holding in

so much heat.
We lived inside that firewall
for a long time, it was

our little box with a crank you could wind up and we
would open our mouths and sing —the nightingale boy and I.
Sang where no one could hear, until

utterly heartsick we threw open the doors and
went outside in the ferns and learned
to love each other.

Or if I went out alone it was
to the street with catalpa trees and long
catkins of cottonwoods. It is possible

to walk down the centerline in moonlight
when all has quieted and the neighbors' lights
have gone out, utterly lost

in the dark crosshatches of branches.
Once the shadow of a pothole proved
to be a porcupine, gathering its coat of shards

and shuffling away.
My hands are pearlskin. My feet
grow hair and claws inside their slippers.

Yes, I tell you,
I am out here —

Dear Body,

    Please let my breath be released, my chest rise and fall. Let energy flow in and around me, unaccountably golden, a river laying down a fibrous sheen.

    Don't you feel how the muscles mold around clots of resistance like a melting brook? Or feel when the sinews turn elastic that you become energy, a softened spun sugar or a honeycomb?

    Every movement is a physical landmark, each vertebrae a homing bee. My backbone pivots like a calculus, approaching some balance it never quite reaches. How motion can become a pure mathematics, if it were not our lives I was speaking of,

        this fusion of tangents, this sweetness and flow—

As if

among ancient ruined temples   roots
spill from the lip of a great courtyard
         formed

of enormous outcrops   home to
      shagbark hickory   mountain laurel   lichen   fern.

Trees   the first inhabitants
            with lightning bolt branches
      consciousness fixed
               in space.   Windows

torn from the walls   wind sweeping
                  from room to room
                                          wind
that takes my breath away   woods
      breathing in
                  sighing out.

Leaves float
            in front of our eyes   as if
on water   extend down

as far as we can see   into the shadows
            schools of fish
      trees gently waving below us   like kelp   the great

sheer-sided sea ledges studded
with quartz.

A breeze slides lightly   across a face.
      It could be rock
                  it could be yours.

What is it like to live in this body, to live in yours

This electric net, this school of fish urging a cinching bag.
        Gravity sinking.

Water presses her full weight against me. My bed of sand.

A wave pulses — the serpent with his glittering skin, my body
        the serpent, my skin
        prickling with eyes.

Your eyes on me. The eyes of stars watching from their nodes
        in the celestial nets.

Sky, ground, water, pressing against us and against each other.
        Us pressing against each other. The rubies in Indra's
        web.

Ancient peoples orienting by constellations and along lines of
        energy between sky, body, sea and stone. We extend
        our hands.

All connected, all sailors casting our nets.

Boulders sleep on the shoreline, constellated, huddled close.
        Their humped backs guide us in the cold streaming air.
        Their connections to each other, to the dreaming web.

Our bodies deeply pressing: muscle and fascia reaching around
        blockages, time passing through us like a sieve.

And mirrored in the water, minnows swim up to kiss the air.

The sea advances

and retracts. It plays
with me like a cat, says
I could sweep you away with one brush of this hand, and
Do you love me? Won't you take me back?

Sand foams down the faces of the slow-breaking
dunes. The breakers,
they break my heart with their long slow drifts.

I peer into the water — To behold. To hold this sight
in my hands, have my hands try to cast it down
on paper —

A distant curve of beach ripples, gathers itself
like a shawl and vanishes.

No lighthouse anymore. No focal point, no goal, no plan, no
narrative arc — the story founders
and comes to a stop.

Earthbound. Spellbound.

I peer, half-dreaming
through the salt mist and evaporating world,
my fingers weaving stories
out of foam.

Dear Woods,

Thank you for showing us the wind, that airy ocean —
how it tosses the frothy heads of pines. The nonhuman calls
itself to order — wood gnats swampwater. I didn't know we
could come back here, so unexpected and alive, not like the
news of constant dying.

O woods, I should say we hadn't been paying attention,
we were lost and not ourselves in the damp lungs of sky and
needle. The distant whine of machinery, the path we were
on not leading to a satisfying conclusion. And some kind of
meandering discussion overhead between your trees, with their
large ears, their expanding hearts. We could mimic them listening
inward, opening outward if we stand here long enough,

if the center holds —

13 lines tied to the wind

the red squirrel runs right towards us then straight up a tree
how surprised he is   how strange
to stand in the middle of a wood not knowing what we are

the wind will not stop blowing
it is not put off by the jibber of news   it is not tied to a profit
              it is simply unspooling
I could mimic it   be birdsong or the red hurricane of fur
when I say wind I really mean voices   I really mean the yellow
              deathcaps rising out of leafmeal
I'm asking you to listen
I'm asking to see how leaves underfoot lay down their bodies
              as a sentence
I try to read but I understand only what I already know

the wind tells us to keep moving
set intention aside   do what we have to do   birds also singing
in the last fused hours of daylight

Bear Swamp sequence

They must
love each other to be
so entwined, trees
whose roots
embrace, muscular
as pythons.

Straight trunk with a seam
stitched up its side, and
fused to its root the stub
of a hollowed-out stump
—brother long dead, the scar
still alive.

~ ~

Cut copper birch
sprouts a dozen
small shoots
rooted in rock
on the side
of an outcrop,
stubborn as anything
that walks this earth.

~ ~

I scrunched through leaf fall
to a sheer cliff face
of peeling lichen, intaglio
of root and branch
overlooking a cleft
running down to the bowl
of a marsh.
          A chipmunk
was as noisy as I, a gray squirrel
also—nothing could move
without announcing itself.
I heard footsteps of something—
upsweep of energy, wind
coming in—leaves giving voice
in a single breath.

~ ~

Gold beech
Yellow birch
A pond mirroring
A mackerel sky
That mirrors
The disk of water
The life of fish
The mind
Turns inward
The voice
Turns inward
I am here
Not there
This is how it is

Cascade

Like tangled hair over stone, roots
    hold trees against a stream. The current loosens
its gorgeous fall, braids and unbraids
    against the rock while roots draw water
to the crown, a fountain and a glory.

    The falls pull water downward
from their spring, the spring
    rises and overflows; leaves
push outwards; the weeping willow
    greens. Cascades swell with rain and spill
their shimmering ringlets down, fall
    and fall all summer long until trees
let down their hair and leaves
    are loosed, lips call sap
back to the earth and all
    stands dark and silent.

Frost grows, the current
    swirls and slows under lacey ice
but does not stop. A tree's heart
    does not freeze in its quiet
sleep. So close and so
    far under. I lay
my hand on root
    and rock. I dip
my hand in water
    and the sap
wells up.

Praise song

In the sea-wind's turbulent currents;
in the roiling breakers and rolling clouds, air full of dipping
        and yawing swallows;
among the dunes stacked one against the other in long
        breakings of sand;
and waves pressing tight against them to yield up their bodies —
sweeping, redistributing, plowing under, sanding
again and again to a perfect
untouched plane —

Sharing the rolling breath with red-winged blackbirds;
the rolling embrace of the twisting oaks, elephantine,
        whirlwinded;
the sun pouring down on the shining grasses, the shining water,
on beach plums, asters, oak seedlings, and the painted
turquoise stone in the oak crook
tenderly placed —

Seablood, sun-soil, flux; the cedars
stunted and spreading their deepest greenest swirls
in ones and threes, all blowing, transitory— this—this
is what love is —

Dear Nightingale Boy,

When I saw how fast my life could flow, I held on to myself, then reached for you. We flew hand in hand over dark streets and city blocks, the park with its nighttime maples, the fields laid low by the deep hand of soil—

How can we ever know what is coming? The branches bud, the buds leaf out, leaves explode into summer, and fall tumbles golden over our shoulders.

We could be beings cloaked in gold, we could be creatures arrayed in fur, the nose leading ours lives forward. Into the surging wind we cry *Come on, come on* but we cannot see what the future beholds in its compound insect eye.

It's enough to breathe: this, then this. I embrace myself,

I reach for you—

The boulders of Lyell Canyon

I name them Upright, Lengthwise, Split
Down the Middle: these granites strewn
like milky stars. You could orient by them, find
your way through creek, meadow, and wood.
This one is here, and that one is there, its neighbor
next to both, old friends grinding down shards
of philosophy. It could take a million years
to see the argument to conclusion, points
split finer and finer, rubbed to a sheen
into pebbles, then to sand in an hourglass.
They record the course of floods, huddle
together beneath parent slopes where they
were wrenched and scraped by glaciers, shaped
and molded by teachers of ice, which explains
their patience and hardness, having been milled
so interminably slowly to an exacting rule.
Now they languish, sun seeping into feldspars
and micas, into the quartzes until they quiver
with pure excitation—in heat and cold, wind
and stillness, through minutes and millennia,
and still radiate impassiveness.

Just underfoot

A tapping in our bodies tells us
an owl is watching, or who is coming before they arrive.

We feel the bleached moon's half-open eye, hear
the man in his grief-dream call to the lion to eat him

and the lion invites him home.
In the house, a tub with a clawed foot,

clamshell with soap, wallpaper snarled
with vines and heather. A woman sleeps

on a pillow of whitened antler, her baby buried
on a swan's wing. We walk the halls

to where the lion pads, and a vine
winds twelve yards underground like a railing

to reach the Iron Age. Naked foot
impressed in siltstone. Even deeper,

the two front hooves of an aurochs stride
side by side like brothers. A man's

freed thighbone—
it could be ours.

Everyone here is a guest

Another life
    takes form from the dead tree's body,
        its limbs a scaffold

for fungus curlicued
    as petticoats, orange
        as apricots.

Look at our moist, our
    suck. We kiss
        to take possession, embrace

to gather world into ourselves, each of us
    frilled, rilled
        all fingers and mouth —

The hoards spill in
    for a rollicking fiesta,
        feeding, fruiting, decomposing

festering.
    The table is spread, the body
        throws open its doors —

Dear Winterwood,

     Winter's coming, did you hear? Five rivers of sap recede from the tree, there is one ear listening, one eye looking out, and a silence at the center of the wood

                      where my heart is —

tzee-wheeee — our rippling muscles racing forward —great sliding hills of air!
Luffs and waves!

Dear dear Miracles,

How can I understand what it is to be so tiny and with
such wings? Could I believe in a chickadee joy?

I hear your rapid wing beats, puncturing the air above me
like sewing machines, see the straight stitch you lay from tree to feeder
and back again, like feathered shuttles. And if you ever paused, what
creviced landscape would those sharp eyes make of me?

I don't know what to say to you —

But I can see why you ally with the titmice, the
woodpeckers and nuthatches — all flock as one against the
hawks, against the cats and kestrels. In the bitter winter, you flock
in a ball of down and trembling, making heat against the night,
against the hunger that will take you down, flocking as a prayer
against the destruction my kind leaves on any given morning.

> *tzee tzee we*
> *rise as one to search the iced bark, the husks and lichen,*
> *for spiders and seed stored from the Age of Summer—*
> *we, no bodies, only feathers and mind, the tickings*
> *we telegraph between us — we*
> *are here-here, we*
> *the winged ones,*
> *we.*

I offer up these seeds to help a few get through the cold, the seeds
  of my contrition.

I remain my inadequacy—

Forcing forsythia

Why wait till spring?
Put the cut branches early into water
and watch them bloom.
That is the way with them:
water, sap, a vase.

This house is altogether too small.
The wings are beating inside my ribs
asking for release,
saying *now*, not tomorrow.

Already those yellow starbursts
are nubbling my mind,
twigs too swollen
to be endured: *here, here, look at me!*
If I were a bee—

Just this

Finally the sap
begins to flow and peepers eager
in tree-cities start up a thousand tiny
rhythmic saws, a thousand quarter-teaspoons
of delirium spooned out drop by drop
in hemidemisemiquavers of frog
belly, frog sperm, frog spawn, frog
joy and jelly, messaged across woodlands
to waiting lovers: *Here here here*
I am the tiny green throats declare, not in
flowers still fisted tight in soil, not in oil-
warmed airless walls but here
with full-cheeked slapping thighs
loosed into the waiting darkness, voicing urges
untongued all winter long *this, just this.*

Open window

It's gripping my pixilated screen,
a wren singing *doobilee-*

doobilee-do, what-would-we
what-would-we do? We jump up

from the table — it veers by, ephemeral
of feather and wing

pummeling our ears, those sad
stiff muscles, sings
lightness of bone, its eye on seeds and bugs, all

black shining O's — O of eye O
of bug, the delicate

leaf a doublet, a flower's stamen
a straw to drink from. What a gift,
my tiny beauty—   I tell you

I want to live.
I'm tired of being bored and logy
and now

this bird has pried open
the box we live in and poured in

something like joy, like steam
gemmed with rainbow

From elbow to hand to window and then
farewell O wren farewell — dusk air

streams in, the curtains pulled, the night
unwrapped around us, heads dizzying
in a bird feather bed

our shoulder blades
quivering and aching.

Green ghazal

It's the hardest color to mimic, a thousand shades, this green.
Have you ever seen such gifts? Ever-changing evergreen.

Hay-scented ferns unfurl into banners. Come in — see
our dyed ostrich feathers in moss, sage, lime, and apple-green.

Why haven't I been praising the heavens again? Show me
where they are! I'm lost in the ferns, in whirlwinds of green.

I dreamed up twelve happy new lines — I'll send them to you.
Like jades on a necklace these glorious gems, still green.

What, are we blind? Even potatoes have eyes that see
in the dirt, and look! in the old pine, a gray peregrine.

Wherever we go, the hawk follows. Wherever you breathe,
it's spring; I'm shaking out my winter socks, all wintergreen!

Here's a whole aisle of scarves, what a feast! Are you always
so inarticulate, so stumbling, so utterly green?

See for yourself how raucously brazen these merchants can be!
Not all the spangles in my hair could rival that green.

Have I learned nothing? Janet's name means *gift*, but all names
are emeralds tossed from the heavens, showers of greenest-green.

Serenade

I tell you, I have such fingers. They talk
and they strut. They bud pink-pronged corals

at the bottom of my arms.
They are writing revolutions that no one

has ever heard of, the whorls deeply studied, the texts
memorized. When I think they're sleeping I find

they're actually star-nosed moles groping forward,
thumbprints on their foreheads which on starless nights

blossom into eyes. Fingers! They used to talk
by telephone, but now they beam over the radical

ether. One day they became starlings that swooped
together as of one mind, and for a moment I thought

I had control. Later I caught them wriggling
in sheer joy because who could stop that wild

tap and thump in the night, dreams
flowing ten rivers strong. Sometimes I wake

with a sensation of struggling underwater, sentences
plastered to my lips and forehead, but then

they rescue me, those ten little baritones,
crooning the words down and pasting them to the page.

Sometimes

a poem will split open in my hands like milkweed.
Sometimes I spread the long grass apart to see   .
the ridged promise of an iris,
    furred blue tongue drawing the literate bees.

The dance & journey come on me, I am stung.
Over the flowertops, through the mosslands,
following a map given to me by strangers:
my life depends on it now.

The hive swirls dark around the mind,
    glittering in the peripheral vision, & laced
        with dripping honey

        word with no name, the stone in the god's mouth
        The world says: *eat of me and die*

        & so
           I leave myself —

Dear Chagall,

      People look everywhere in darkened rooms, faces split between goat and rooster, clock and moon. They line up with horns and cymbal, preparing to negotiate their condition with God.

      In the froth of a rooster's tail feathers, two lovers kiss, and later we discover a woman blossoming — he buries himself in the flowers. She is floating above the crowd, watching someone
                  watching someone else. O dear artist

take my brush, guide my hand — *but my art*
                was really an insanity —
            wild bellflowers in the layered drifts.

                    We remain, sweetly lost—

In the fullness

of late May the sun sags mired
in its own roundness; tired

the day sighs and drags its heels,
tugging the unwilling emergent eves.

Beads of metallic song weep
off the hermit thrush's beak.

Lilacs grow potent in late afternoon
and we more mothlike, fluttering and aswoon

with inarticulate desire:
summer comes on us like a brush fire,

until the sun melts down completely,
the last word said, and we have gently

placed our parents in their royal graves
and suffered dreams of darkness, wave upon waves—

All around us lie our wealth and ease—
into our laps drop dusky nectarines.

August

By mid-morning the air stumbles.
The sun's a hazy incandescence,

crows saw away at the silence,
the garden burgeons up in sweaty umbels.

Summer squash invades the lettuce,
tomatoes are too fat to stand, the beans

strangle while gold-green beetles
wrest leaves into lattices.

Everyone grabs while the heat lasts;
the sun oozes with juice,

the whole structure sags.
By afternoon, thunderheads bruise

the horizon— violence heightens;
summer swells, and overripens.

I am moving in the deep

space above the water again, above
the roof, above the field where daylilies
bend their heads to summer and hummingbirds
sing into the curved ears of the beebalm.
The soul moves outward from the body,
then collects itself in armfuls of air.
Above the sunny fields a shining
detritus spins on fourfold wings
and darning tails, and clouds of gnats
cast compound nets around us. It is possible

to see all this and not be dead. The joy
pours in like grateful gulps of water
after a long absence. I have missed you
more than you could ever know, and now
I find you here, on this day that I am alive
with the skysoul clattering between maples
and leafsouls tethered to the long woodhair
of the old world-tree, its scabrous toes
in the earth. So it is for us and today
we sing of it.

Dear Gray Light,

Can you hear the wren, flinging its joyous rouse into the dim? The world hangs half in slumber, rolls over— Oh dear world, deep resonant blue — these breathing lungs, these armfuls of air — I rise to my feet, leaving my sleeping lover there.

Who am I not married to? Who has not forsaken their deepest ardors to slip out under the blanching flesh of heaven, keys in hand, road opening darkly? The earth wheels underneath, car rocking like a cradle — I see the sky's great rafters suspended above, beams of galaxy and sunrise.

I remain, restless wandering —

In the Provincelands

On the cusp of a dune in the middle of dunes in the middle of the sea.

A hand turns the page, the ocean overturns the land.

The land picks up & moves grain by grain across the highway.

And you & I who have traveled
        are here in a swirl of compass grass.

One ridge after another floats into the binocular lens until we reach
        the edge
beyond which

there is only blue: sky-fused waves, sea serpents
        foaming & half crazy.

We surely are lost, but down
is still down. The Lucy G. sank tied up at the pier & lay there
patrolled by squid, embossed with barnacles, seaweed
                        tugging at her rigging in the tide.

You could look straight down
        on her decks & derricks, not so tidy now.

Look up:
a heady diaphanous robe. Dusk settling, sun giving way to languor,
        your warm brown thigh. A person

could touch—here—wipe the freckling sand from its curve.
From the cleft between

a throaty motor starts up, whines & lifts
into the air: ultralight climbing a steep hill, east or south or west,
                    light blurring into indigo.

Two figures,
        you & I dozing, backs to a biting wind,

wondering when coyotes emerge from their beech forest dens,

wondering about safe haven, safe landing, what else
will shake itself from sand

        to rise up, circling.

Dear Swans,

Here on the shore of a tidal inlet you seem to sleep, pale white against powdery fog. Your sinuous curve of beach and neck. Your lenticular bodies, neck draping over wing, wing folded over breast.

Nothing was ever said about Leda and the sea, how her hair was twined with rope and her breast a bell buoy. How you found her floating face down in the surf and dragged her ashore, fans of lacy foam spreading like nerves.

The deep powerful breakers, your foaming chests coming in fierce and fast. I could get burned in the mist, I could be washed away, neck helpless in a swan's beak.

I grasp at air with my hands, I drown.

The spell is cast — people hazed over in the surf doused with swan feather, and pale unbelievers sprawled out watching from the beach. I of the white shirt, I the swanling swimming in an ocean of salt.

Nothing can stop the tears, not the fog nor the sand nor terns cutting the air with their scissors, nor the dancers nor the music.

I remain your applause—

Forecast

Sunset lights the wharf's
    thin strip of shops, whose
distant windows glint
    rose and coral,
a wavering scrim
    between harbor and sky.
Tinny calliopes, a stiffening
    breeze, pennants
flapping on halyards
    beyond which lies
the open ocean.
    And when we walk out onto

the pier itself, the mirage becomes
    as lifelike as our own
bodies. A refugee city
    in water, Atlantis
putting brave face to the
    sea rising
below our feet. Reflections
    of trawlers, tour boats,
and yacht from
    Bikini all quiver
as if lacquered
    in mercury.
The Barco de Jesus putts in
    on sky-blue
paint, and Probable Cause
    lists to port,
stripped down to a cement-

gray casing. Blessed
voyagers,
       everyone battens down
in the oily
       calm as if there were
no tomorrow —

The ferry arrives
       spinning its radar's silent
eye, and the sun—
       now a pin-hole —
exposes us.
       But two old
fishermen
       banter back and forth across
the wharf—all the hours
       they'd spent out there
searching the watery
       sunlit porches for cod. Nightly
they walk over the sea
       trailing and dreaming
their endless nets. The wind
       goes slack, skeins
of dark clouds
       gathered in its hands.

Dear Paper Wasps Who Feed on Flowers,

What can I do to absolve the past among these endless piles of luggage? And who helped me out of my pain that was my whole life, and now expects me to save the world?

Today I saved ten sunflower seeds for next year. Part of today's lunch for tomorrow. My energy, for tomorrow. My creative insights and my outrage, for another day. I ate a fine blueberry off a thin bush crying for sun.

But when one of you got stuck inside my window, I showed him the slit under the screen to freedom, nudging him with a finger. I did it without thinking, without wondering what or why.

Is it possible you and your family will prod us with your stingers out the narrowing exit?

We remain, humankind—

Taking it in at 800 miles an hour

On our backs, side by side, we look
straight up at a field of stars and swirls
of galaxies. I try to take it in, this planet's
ferocious whirling with a load of humans
on its back, seven billion of us
cutting and clearing, the way once
my dog's short hair jittered and swam, his skin
crawling with fleas.

Too many of us, too many
mouths and ceaseless copulations.
Desires, cryings, indifferences,
all of it human. How can it be
as we are taught, that each of us
is a gift?
I look over where your face
blurs in darkness and a rush
comes over me. Truly
you are my gift, and when
I am kind to myself
maybe I could be yours also, our bodies given
to manifest our simple hopes, to ride

this streaking ball of home wrapped
in black flannel, pricked through
by stars. And right now,
how many thousands
of couples are staring up,
whispering to each other
how lucky we are?

Ballinskelligs

Dark birds heft the luminous air in wingfuls,
the sea is a shimmer of fish scale and lead,
and The Bull and The Cow lie suspended
on a strip of bright water, heavy as flatirons.
Islands, water, salt, and cloud
all flowing stardust.

Sunrise, sunset — we mark
the wheeling seasons like iron age people,
view tombs where the dead are buried
in alignment with the stars; and in my body
the iron, oxygen, calcium, and carbon
all tug for home.

Last night there was mist, and the moon had set.
Out where no land was, lights floated
on the horizon — lighthouse, star, ship? They seemed
not to exist, with nothing to pin them to
except darkness, a fold of the cosmic cloak
brushing the edges of Ballinskelligs Bay.

You say
your head is too full. Mine also.
I need stillness and silence, the spinning
to stop. I want to be seated in my bones
to befriend these bits of blown apart stars
churning inside me. Stardust to stardust,

each to each. The newborn lambs
bleat after their mothers, and I'm homesick.

We have traveled so far in these bodies,
worried too much and carried too much.
You glance at me and I gaze back —
a rising wind — sharp, salt.

Flying at night

Somewhere in the dark North Atlantic
fishermen winnow the sea until nothing is left
except sadness. The fields
never lay fallow, scraped to the bones
of shimmering fish.

A curtain of snow
sweeps across waves so thick
you couldn't see your nose, if you were there and not
three miles high, blind, ear-budded,
breathing by umbilicus
to the carbon fiber webbing.

Out of mind, flocks of seabirds float,
scattered plashes of white, and polar bears
hitch rides on waxy slicks from Greenland
to Baffin Island.

The sea could be pewter,
a length of silk stretched over
our waiting bones. The sleeper
gathers a dark shawl of bubbles
around her shoulders, the edge of surf
under her chin. The dream becomes

thirst in an ocean of salt,
what we have always desired, held dear
to our hearts. I could write all night
trying to knit what our hearts divulge
and our dreams ensnare, while far below
whales sleep with one eye open
and the other eye closed.

Dear Old House,

You know the way spring weather swings hot and cold? Wet and dry? Swings and swings. High and low, sweet chariot, it swings.

Will our houses grieve after we are gone? — all that creative beauty, our dark intuition. The music. The human compassion. I have lived here for decades and never noticed. All I wished for was to be somewhere else, to be somebody else.

But dear old house, here I am with you, at home.

I dreamed this was only half the world. I dreamed a whale came up and ate
so many frantic Jonahs she released them back to land, each with their own message.

I had a message, I tried to write it down but the heavens unleashed the flood. The trees crashed down and shattered across the washouts. Oh home, all four directions away from you were closed. All four roads undercut to bedrock, cut on the bias, disassembled, a succession of anvils.

O dear house, can you hear the wren battering against the screen door, hoarsely twittering? She wants in. Now.

Every house is an ark, every house is an ark. Every creature frantic

for one small piece of ground.

And guess what, the Army Corps of Engineers just arrived. There is nothing they can't fix. No one can build a dam better than they. Civilization reassembled dam by dam, culvert by culvert.

Anything not civilization is trucked or cut away.

Dear Dear House,

I had to stop writing

and now it's summer. The heat is burgeoning, cicadas start up their sawing, the grass grows long and tufted under a gentle sky. Coneflowers, black-eyed Susans, beebalm. The phoebe under the deck raises her second brood, the Carolina wren waking me at dawn.

Sweet endless time.

Do you know how much I love this season, full summer laziness? Is it possible that I belong in the world? That the world I dream of is already here?

I remain longing—

NOTES

pg 33: Much of this poem draws from *Time Song: Searching for Doggerland* by Julia Blackburn

pg 47: italicized text drawn from Marc Chagall's *My Life*.

pg 50: Thanks to Joy Harjo for the title and first line of this poem.

pg 59: Although paper wasps largely eat insects, depending on the time of year and other factors they also drink nectar in flowers and can act as pollinators.

ABOUT THE AUTHOR

JANET MACFADYEN is the author of three full-length poetry collections, most recently *State of Grass* (Salmon Poetry 2024) and *Waiting to Be Born* (Dos Madres Press 2017), along with four chapbooks. Honors include a Massachusetts Cultural Council grant, a 7-month Fine Arts Work Center fellowship in Provincetown, and a Cill Rialaig residency in Ireland, in addition to prizes for the *Naugatuck River Review* and *Common Ground Review* annual contests. She has been nominated for the Best of the Net, Pushcart, and Forward prizes. Recent work appears in *Slant, The Closed Eye Open, The Hopper, The High Window, Scientific American, Wordpeace*, and several Writing the Land anthologies. She is the managing editor of Slate Roof Press, a poetry chapbook collaborative. In earlier lives, she majored in geology and worked for a meteorological instrument manufacturer.

https://www.facebook.com/janet.macfadyen

ACKNOWLEDGEMENTS

Grateful thanks to the editors of the following publications in which these poems first appeared, some in different form and under different titles:

50/50: Poems & Translations by Womxn over 50 (QuillsEdge Press anthology): Dear Nightingale Boy
Four Corners: In the fullness
Garlic Arts Festival 2024 Anthology: Dear Gray Light; How I walk into my life
*Honoring Nature (*Nature/Culture): 13 lines tied to the wind; Bear Swamp sequence; Scrub oak, pitch pine
Meat for Tea: We find ourselves born here
Migrations (Nature/Culture anthology): Flying at night
Osiris: Everything we thought familiar emerges utterly strange; Sometimes
*Pandemic Poetry and Prose (*Straw Dog Writer Guild): Dear Woods
Persimmon Tree: Love letters to the wild
Rosebud: Dear Winterwood
Scientific American: The boulders of Lyell Canyon
SGEM World Science (SWS) blog: Cascade
Slant: Taking it in at 800 miles per hour
Soul Lit: I am moving in the deep; As if; Green ghazal; Open window
Sweet: In the Provincelands
The Closed Eye Open: Forecast
The High Window: Praise song
The Hopper: Just this
The Montague Reporter: August, Just underfoot, Everyone here is a guest
Tiny Seed Literary Journal: Forcing forsythia
White Stag (#spirit): What is it like to live in this body, to live in yours; I am a parched forest

For the full Dos Madres Press catalog:
www.dosmadres.com

www.ingramcontent.com/pod-product-compliance
Lightning Source LLC
Chambersburg PA
CBHW021129130626
46554CB00002B/928